TEN SCENIC WALKS

AROUND

ROSEDALE, FARNDALE

AND

HUTTON LE HOLE

by

J. Brian Beadle

First published in Great Britain in 1999 by Trailblazer Publishing
(Scarborough)

www.trailblazerbooks.co.uk

ISBN 1 899004 29 7

Trailblazer
Unit 1
R/O 9 Market Place
Pickering
YO18 7AE

MAPS

The maps in this book are not to scale and are for guidance only. They do not
accurately portray the right of way. It is the readers responsibility not to stray
from the right of way and it is strongly advised that you take an Ordnance Sur-
vey map with you on the walk.

WARNING

Whilst every effort has been made for accuracy neither the publisher nor the
author bear responsibility for the alteration, closure or portrayal of rights of
way in this book. It is the readers responsibility not to invade private land or
stray from the public right of way. All routes in the book should be treated
with respect and all precautions taken before setting out. Any person using in-
formation in this book does so at their own risk.

CONTENTS

ABOUT ROSEDALE

Nestling in the beautiful valley of Rosedale lies the village of Rosedale Abbey. Situated in the centre of the North York Moors National Park the village is thirty four miles from Scarborough on the east coast and thirty two miles from the City of York inland. The dale of Rosedale is eight miles in length and has a wide variation of scenery. There are wooded hillsides, rocky crags, streams, bogs, moorland and cultivated farming land. There are small shops, a bakery and pleasant cafes in the village as well as two excellent pubs. A cup of tea at the Abbey Tea Rooms or a stronger drink in the garden of the Milburn Arms is a pleasant way to while away a summers afternoon if it is too hot for walking.

Rosedale Church Site Of The Abbey

The village of Rosedale Abbey inherits its name from the Priory which was founded in the 12th century and supported nine nuns and a Prioress. There were a few lay workers, mainly farmers and shepherds and the Priory had around twelve sacks of wool for sale annually from their flock of sheep. The Priory survived until Henry 8th called for a suppression of the Monasteries and the Priory at Rosedale was destroyed in the 16th century. The church that stands there today is well worth a look, as are the last remains of the abbey which must have been impressive in its day. Please put some money in the honesty box to help the upkeep of the church.

It is hard to believe that this small corner of North Yorkshire on the edge of the bleak North York Moors could have played such an important part in our industrial heritage. Although the Romans brought improved farming methods to the area and the French set up a glass house making goblets, tumblers, flasks etc. in 1567, it was the demand for iron from industrial Teesside in the early 1800's that started a revolution in the dale. No small scale operation that the Romans or Iron Age people developed but a large and vigorous industry fuelled by the insatiable demand for iron for the developing world. Rosedale

became a thriving mining community with iron ore mines opening on both sides of the valley and on the hills surrounding the adjacent valley of Farndale. The population of Rosedale swelled from a few hundred to over five thousand when mining was at its peak. Men came from all over England and Ireland for a chance to earn the relatively high wages that the dangerous job paid.

Battersby Junction

Some even travelled across Europe from Italy to be part of the North Yorkshire mining boom. It is easy to imagine the scene in the 1800's as hard faced miners gambled their money away and became drunk. Frequent fights broke out as miners, railway staff and hangers-on jockeyed for position.

Rosedale boasted a railway around both sides of the dale for the transportation of the iron ore to industrial Teesside. The steam train would puff and pant its way around the dale side then make its way across Blakey ridge via the Farndale mines to meet the North Eastern Railway branch line from Battersby Junction. At the opposite end of the dale at Rosedale Bank Top there was a huge chimney which could be seen for miles around. This chimney, now demolished, was the part of the winding engine which hauled the trains up the incline from mines in the Hollins Farm area. As the demand for iron declined the mining operations closed one by one. What was once a thriving industry was becoming an expensive, dwindling embarrassment to the owners. After the pit closures the only thing of value became the slag from the calcinating kilns which was recovered and processed. The railway finally closed in June 1939 leaving the old railway track bed on which we can enjoy a scenic walk around the dale.

WALKING IN MINERS FOOTSTEPS

*R*osedale Abbey is a quiet village with a good pub, tea shop and bakery. It wasn't nearly so quiet in the 19th century when the iron ore industry was booming. Hundreds of hard working, hard drinking and boisterous miners inhabited the dale quarrying iron ore to supply developing Teesside. The walk takes us into mining country where a few relics still stand. An even earlier industry survived in the 16th century – glass making. The route takes us past the site of this industry which was carried out by the French! Returning over the high moors the view into Rosedale is outstanding.

THE FACTS

Distance - 8 miles/12.8 km
Time - 3 hours
Start - Free but small car parks in
Rosedale, grid ref. 725959
Maps - OS Landranger 100
Terrain - Boggy at times, steep downhill
Refreshments - Good pub, tea rooms, bistro and bakery at Rosedale.

The Route

*S*tart the walk from one of the two free car parks adjacent to the Milburn Arms pub and head off towards the Abbey Stores and Tea Rooms then past the Post Office. Near the entrance to the Rosedale Caravan Park go right across the bridge signed to Rosedale Chimney Bank. The road climbs steeply for a short way to the White Horse Farm Hotel. Turn left at the bridleway sign across the hotel car park to exit on a farm road at the rear. You pass several cottages, a farm and a pottery studio as you go. Shortly, after the track falls it rises to Hollins Farm and a rickety old barn. This is where the first Rosedale iron ore mine was situated. You can see some remains of the quarry on the hill on the right. Walk in the direction of the bridleway sign pointing uphill through a pair of old stone gateposts. Follow the wall on the left around to the left keeping on the narrow track, do not take the wider track up the hill. Keep on the obvious path which is occasionally boggy and rocky. Ignore all offerings of other paths   off   to the left.   Eventually you arrive   at a   plaque commemorating the site of the 16th century French glass works.

The path climbs to the right shortly onto the moor then falls again to High Askew Farm. Watch your head along here there are low tree branches. At the farm road go right over the hill to reach a gate. Do not go through the gate but turn right onto a wide track which climbs onto the moor. This track twists and turns as it climbs for 3 miles (4.8 km) over the Grouse moor. You will see lots of nesting Curlews on your way as well as other wildlife, please keep dogs on leads. The higher you climb the better the views across the moors to the green valleys and ridges all around. Near the end of the climb you will see Anna Cross which crashed to the ground several years ago, now thankfully rebuilt it stands prominent as a landmark on these high moors once again. Soon you reach the road at Rosedale Chimney Bank top. The old mine workings are all around you with the stone calcinating kilns prominent in the hillside. Return to Rosedale along the wide grass verge, but beware of the traffic. It is hard on the knees all the way to the bottom of this extremely steep hill.

Rosedale

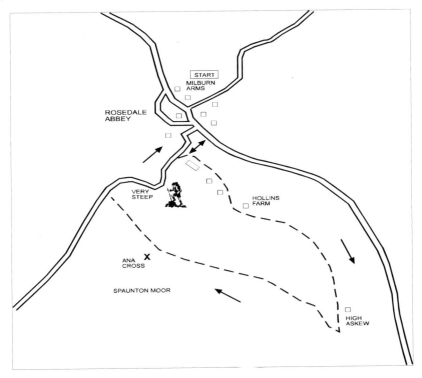

OVER NORTHDALE RIGG

Northdale Rigg protects Rosedale from the severe north east winds. We cross the Rigg on our way to an old mining area before walking over the wild Hamer Moor to head back to the shelter of the dale. The view from the rigg across the dale to Spaunton Moor and Rosedale Bank Top are outstanding.

THE FACTS

Distance - 8 miles/13 km
Time - 3½ hours.
Start - Rosedale Abbey, grid ref. 725960
Maps - OS Landranger 100.
Terrain - Moorland paths. Undefined in places over Rigg
Refreshment - Two cafes and two pubs in Rosedale Abbey

The Route

Start from the small car park behind the Milburn Arms. If full there is another park adjacent to the pub. Follow the public footpath sign through the gate at the rear of the car park. Cross the field staying close to Northdale Beck on your left. Keep following the beck crossing several stiles on the way until you arrive at a signpost. Continue straight ahead here following the sign for 'concessionary path'. The path follows the river then after two more stiles you reach a bridge and a gate to a signpost. Keep straight on still following the bridleway sign.

At the road turn right and in about half a mile immediately after a house used as a stable, turn right through a gate at the bridleway sign. Go uphill to climb onto the moor via a gate.

Take the left fork now and still climbing head for another gate onto open moorland. Soon you cross a wide track but keep on your narrow path through the heather. The track becomes undefined at times, even disappearing altogether. If you head for the shooting butts slightly to your left you will come to a crevice, keep right here and follow the crevice which in winter could be wet. This takes you downhill to a small stream. On the horizon straight ahead you will see mounds of the old workings. This is where you are heading. Cross the stream and you should see a narrow path winding its way through the heather. Follow the line of the wall on the right and when the wall bends to the right keep straight ahead to pass through the middle of the workings. The track then bears right to the road. Cross the road taking the bridleway sign. The wide track soon forks, take the right fork away from the wall. Now for the tricky bit! In about a mile you will pass a pile of stones on the right. Then, in a hundred yards or so look for a wide swathe of grass through the heather leading to a

gate in the wall on your right. If you reach a clump of trees on the right you have gone too far and are trespassing. You must turn right before the small plantation! Pass through the gate in the wall and across a couple of fields to reach a quiet road at the side of a farm. Turn right here and walk along the road for about a mile where at a junction near a derelict farmhouse keep straight ahead, then in a few yards turn right at the public footpath sign. This leads through a pleasant wood rich in bilberries. Follow the obvious path along the edge of the wood and onto the moor, crossing two stiles and a gate. At the road cross a stone stile and turn right then immediately left at the footpath sign. It is downhill now with scintillating views across Rosedale to the old mine workings on the other side of the valley.
Pass through a gate and over a stile to arrive at a signpost. Turn right eventually passing over a large stile on the way to a farm. Go through the farm gate then left to exit onto the road. Follow the minor road to the junction and turn right to head back to Rosedale and the welcoming Milburn Arms.

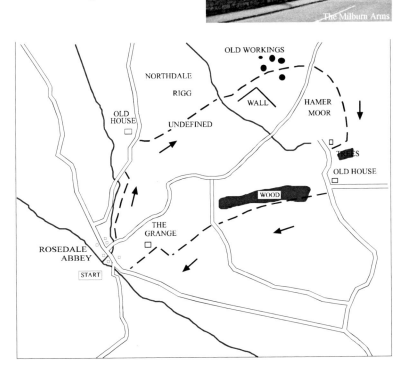

ROSEDALE'S MINERAL RAILWAY

In the middle of the 19th century developing Teesside was hungry for iron ore. Deposits were found at Rosedale and Farndale and a branch line built to transport the ore for processing in the Teesside blast furnaces. A connecting line from Blakey was built around the dale of Rosedale to collect the ore from the mines. On the walk you will pass the old Calcinating kilns which were built to roast the ore. This reduced the water and carbonic acid content before transportation. The mines were closed finally in 1926 and the railway three years later.

Iron ore was processed at Rosedale long before it was needed at Teesside. It is thought to have been smelted in the 12th/13th century. There were several furnaces in a bloomery near Hartoft in medieval days.

NOTE – *The old railway line is not a definitive right of way, walkers are allowed on the route by kind permission of the landowners. Please respect this concession.*

THE FACTS

Distance - 12 miles/19 km
Time - 6 hours
Start - Free but small car parks in Rosedale
grid ref. 725959
Maps - OS Landranger 100
Terrain - Boggy at times, steep uphill from start
Refreshments - Good pub, tea rooms, bistro and
bakery at Rosedale

The Route

Start the walk from one of the two free car parks adjacent to the Milburn Arms pub and head off towards the Abbey Stores and Tea Rooms then past the Post Office. Near the entrance to the Rosedale Caravan Park go right across the bridge signed to Rosedale Chimney Bank. The road climbs steeply and is narrow in places, please take care. Keep on past the ruined Calcinating kilns to a parking area on the right at the top of the hill. Turn right here towards the cottages and follow the cinder track. In about four miles the track passes the Lion Inn.

There is a footpath to the Inn, see walk ten for access. Along the way you will pass many old ruins and industrial remains until you reach the end of the dale. The track bends to the right now and becomes narrow. Take care here as it can be quite boggy. Once past the head take care down a tricky incline on the path at east Rosedale which soon opens out to old railway track again. Ahead of you now in the distance tucked into the hillside the remains of the Calcinating kilns stand proud. The iron ore from the mines was roasted in these kilns to make it easier and lighter to transport. The process left a residue of Calcine dust which at first was tipped down the hillside as waste until, early in the 1920's it was put to commercial use. The track towards the kilns has small subsidence holes in it, watch out for them! Continue along the path past the kilns until more ruined buildings come into view. Go to the left of these buildings and exit by the metal gate then through the right-of-way across the farmyard to the gate opposite. At the end of the farm track turn left onto the tarmac road and follow the signs back to Rosedale Abbey.

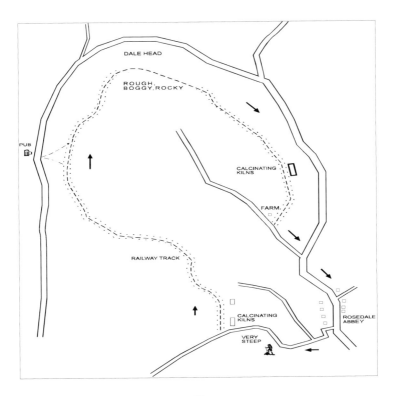

BLAKEY AND THE LION INN

*T*he remote Lion Inn on Blakey Ridge is thought to have been founded by Friars in the 16th century. The Inn increased its trade in the 18th century as farmers from the surrounding dales traded there as corn dealers to horse breeders and owners. Sales connected with farming have played a big part in the history of the Lion inn and there is still an annual sheep sale held there.

When the iron ore mines commenced in the 19th century the whole area of Rosedale and Farndale benefited from the large influx of workers. The Inns flourished and the Lion was no exception being near to the Farndale mines and railway. The Inn now quenches the thirst of weary walkers and travellers where good food and accommodation is always available. This walk passes the door and I suggest you bow to temptation and pass over the threshold to refresh yourselves.

THE FACTS

Distance - 2 miles/ 3½ km
Time -1 hour
Start - Stop at roadside parking area, grid ref. 683989.
Opposite the junction signed to 'Farndale via BlakeyBank'.
Maps - OS Landranger 94 or OS Outdoor Leisure 26
Terrain - Easy walking on good paths
Refreshments - Lion Inn on Blakey Ridge

The Route

Start from the roadside parking area alongside the Hutton le Hole to Castleton road at the 'Farndale via Blakey Bank junction'. At one end and rear of the car park follow the sign 'Footpath to Rosedale'. When you meet the railway line turn left onto it. In about half a mile turn left up a rough, stony track which climbs uphill to the road and the Lion Inn. (If you see a house high above you on the left whilst you are walking along the railway track you have missed the left turn!)

Turn right along the side of the road and pass in front of the Inn keeping it on your left and aim for the standing stone on top of the hill. Unless curiosity gets the better of you there is no reason to visit the stone but keep on the path on the left, then follow the wall round to the left. Keep on the path as it falls down through the heather to eventually reach the old mineral railway track.

Turn left onto the track and keep straight ahead to the gate. Turn left through the gate at the road then cross the main road to return to your transport.

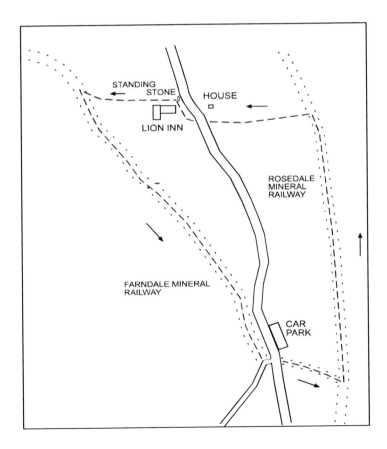

A SHORT WALK TO BELL END

*T**here are many becks and gills running off the surrounding moors into Rosedale, most of the water from them finds its way into the River Seven which grows in stature and power as it leaves the dale to cross Ryedale. The Seven rushes across the dale racing the River Dove on its way from Farndale. Both rivers meet their end as they join together to create an even mightier river, the Rye.***

This walk takes us along one of the tributaries of the Seven, Northdale Beck, then returns close to the Seven as it flows along the dale back to Rosedale Abbey. The walk is almost all field walking and can be quite muddy at times when wet.

THE FACTS

Distance - 3 miles/5 km
Time - 2 hours
Start - Rosedale Abbey. Two small car parks near the
    Milburn Arms. Grid ref. 724960
Maps - OS Landranger 94 or OS Outdoor Leisure 26
Terrain - Easy walking on grassy paths. One short climb
Refreshments – Cafes and Pubs in Rosedale

The Route

S tart from the centre of the village and take the Castleton road. In about 50 yards/metres turn right just before the stone bridge along the signed public footpath. Keep straight ahead along a well used path into a field. Keep Northdale Beck on your left and keeping straight on pass over several stiles and through fields. Eventually arrive at a signpost. Keep straight ahead following the sign along the concessionary path. Soon you arrive at a large gate and a footbridge over Northdale Beck. Cross the bridge then through a small gate to a signpost. Turn left now along the footpath up a steep bank. Continue over the hill through a wood, where you might see lots of Pheasants, to the road. In front of you the hill with the trees on top is Bell Top. Turn left onto this road and head downhill to Bell End and Bell End Farm. Go left at the road junction then in a few yards just before the cottage on the right turn right into a field through a large gate at the footpath sign. Keep close to the hedge on the left and cross the field to a stile into a rough patch of land with a narrow path, watch out for the nettles!

The path leads steeply downhill to the River Seven. Don't cross the river but bear left to a stile with a yellow waymark which leads into a field. Cross the field bearing left uphill for a short while then keep straight ahead on an obvious path which runs parallel to a caravan site. The path eventually enters the caravan site. Keep straight ahead through the site to the recreation field. At

the end of the recreation field look for the footpath sign and waymarks pointing left. Go left here to join the road. Turn left past the glassworks then right at the junction to walk past the toilets to return to Rosedale Abbey village centre.

Rosedale Centre

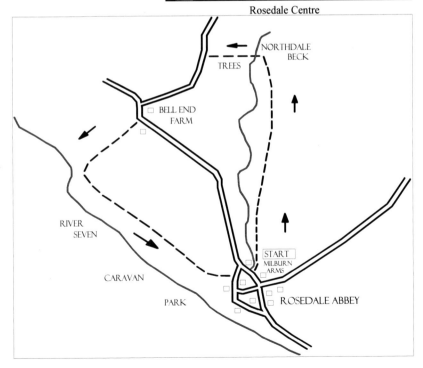

ABOUT FARNDALE

Farndale, famous for its spring daffodils, must be the most beautiful dale in Yorkshire especially when viewed from the heights of Rudland Rigg. Looking across to Blakey Rigg which forms the other side of the dale industrial scars of the ironstone mining days are now well hidden. The only remaining feature apart from a few overgrown hillocks is the track of the ironstone railway which linked up with the Rosedale railway before crossing the side of Blakey Rigg on its way to Bloworth Crossing and on to industrial Teesside. Farndale is a farming community now, mining was only a short period in its long history.

The Hamlets of Farndale are Low Mill and Church Houses, the latter having a pub, the former a post office. There is a small café, the 'Daffy Caffy' a short walk from Church Houses where sustenance is available otherwise food is available at the pub, the Feversham Arms at Church Houses.

In the valley below is the River Dove which takes its water from the surrounding moors and Riggs to flow from a trickle at the dale head to a rush as it leaves Farndale on its way to meet the River Rye and eventually the

mighty River Derwent. The banks of the River Dove are covered by yellow, nodding daffodils in the spring. Millions of flowers in the meadows and woods, the original bulbs planted many years ago by the monks. Try to do walk number eight in the spring to enjoy this golden carpet of wild daffodils. Whilst walking along the banks of the River Dove beware the ghost of Sarkless Kitty who lured her lover to his death in the river. She is said to still appear naked on the river bank trying to lure other young men to their death. The author bears no responsibility for your safety if you should see the beautiful Kitty on your travels and cannot resist her charms!

ABOUT HUTTON LE HOLE

Hutton le Hole is unique amongst the villages of the North York Moors. Its picture postcard looks have inspired many artists, some of whom you will see on the green recording the beauty of the village in oil and watercolour. The old stone cottages with their white paling fences contrast against the green grass kept short by moorland sheep. In the centre of the village is the Ryedale Folk Museum. It has many old buildings re-erected in its grounds and is an intriguing look at country life and its customs. The name Hutton le Hole evolved from Hoton, through Hege-Hoton, Hoton under Heg and Hutton in the Hole. It is thought to have meant 'the place near the burial mounds.' Like Rosedale the French glassmakers came and started a glassworks in the 16th century. It seems that the raw materials for glassmaking were to be found in abundance in the area at the lower end of Douthwaite Dale. The glass they produced was green and made into decorated glasses, goblets and beakers.

Hutton le Hole was affected slightly by the rush for iron ore at the Rosedale mines as some of the miners lived in the village. The population around that time swelled to over five hundred as miners were recruited to work at the top of Rosedale Bank. They probably strode out on the same paths as we enjoy walking on today between Hutton le Hole and Rosedale.

There were several old roads in this area in medieval days, one went from Kirkbymoorside via Hutton le Hole to Rosedale. Not a road as we know it but an earthen track, rutted and most certainly muddy during the wet months. All sorts of goods for everyday use would be carried over the road usually by horse and cart. Another old road went from Farndale up the side of Rudland Rigg from Monket House. It joined the highway on top of the Rigg from Kirkbymoorside along Waingate and across the Rigg.   As   we   walk along this lonely road in summer

Hutton Le Hole

and soak up the magnificent views it isn't hard to imagine what a difficult life, especially in winter, travellers would have had going about their business in medieval days.

HIGH, LOW AND VICTORIA CROSSES

T hree crosses for the price of one here! With the views from Victoria Cross being the jewel. High Cross is situated in a hedge and Low Cross is on the grass verge. Both are said to be markers for visitors on their way to Lastingham Abbey. Although it is said that Low Cross was once the village stocks! Victoria Cross stands high above Lastingham and was erected to commemorate Queen Victoria's Diamond Jubilee. The cross is plain but in fine condition. The view across Lastingham to the moors is outstanding.

THE FACTS

Distance - 7½ miles/12 km
Time - 3½ hours
Start - Village car park at Hutton le Hole
grid ref. 704903
Maps - OS Landranger 94 or OS Outdoor Leisure 27
Refreshment - Pub in Appleton le Moors. Pub at Lastingham. Forge Tea Rooms at Hutton le Hole

The Route

S tart from the village of Hutton le Hole at the village car park. Turn left out of the car park onto the road then left at the road junction to the Ryedale Folk Museum. Turn left again alongside and just past the Museum at the public footpath sign. Pass through a small gate through the car park of the Barn Hotel and exit at the right rear over a stile. In the field bear left parallel to the folk museum buildings and keep straight ahead following a series of waymarks and stiles to soon reach a wood. Climb uphill in the wood to the grass verge and road. Bear right at the road and shortly cross a bridge to a road junction. Go left here to Lastingham. Pass the church and pub then turn right at the sign for Appleton le Moors. As you climb the hill you will see Victoria Cross high up in front of you. At the top of the hill turn right along the grassy bank top to visit Victoria Cross and enjoy the fabulous view. Return to this point then go right signed to Spaunton. Pass through the village and at the sharp right bend go left along a muddy track and through a gate. Keep straight on along this track for about a mile to a crossroads of tracks. Turn left at the footpath sign across a field. After crossing a stile follow the hedge right then left around the field to exit onto the road. Turn right at the road, in a few yards you will see High Cross on your right then as you reach the village Low Cross stands at the junction on the left. In a few yards you arrive at Appleton le Moors. At Appleton Hall on your right take the track signed 'Link' and 'To village sports field' at the rear of the Hall. At a grassy crossroads of tracks go right signed to Spaunton. It is a long uphill drag across the seemingly never ending field track to another grassy crossroads of tracks. Turn left this time as directed by a Public Bridleway and Link sign to a gate. Cross a field and before the track falls downhill turn right into the wood through a gate at the link sign.

Follow the track through the wood eventually exiting onto a wide farm track. At the farm track turn right at the blue waymark, keep straight ahead at all times until the track reaches a field. Follow the hedge round left here onto a wide track which eventually falls downhill to exit onto the road at the entrance to Hutton le Hole. Turn right at the road to walk back into the village and a cup of tea at the Forge Tea Rooms which is on your right.

Hutton Le Hole

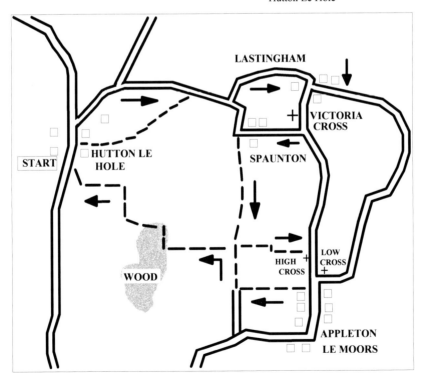

ANA or AINE HOWE CROSS

T *he wilds of Spaunton Moor haven't changed much since the search for iron ore ended in the early 1900's. Only the scars are left as evidence of the area's industrial heritage of its mining days. At Rosedale Bank Top there are some old kilns still standing and evidence of railway tracks. It is at the bank top that you must set off across the moor to visit Ana Cross, albeit in a sorry state the last time I visited it, but now rebuilt. Ana Cross is the tallest on the moors and has been a landmark for hundreds of years guiding lost souls over this bleak terrain. The repaired cross has a new shaft with the original head on top. Lastingham village is worthy of exploration. It boasts a fine pub with good ale and food. It was run by the Curate's wife in the 18th century, she had thirteen children! Was it something in the beer? It could have been, because another strange fact is that the Curate would play the fiddle in the pub to entertain his guests! Whilst you are at Lastingham visit the church which was originally founded by St Cedd who believed there was a strange power on the site. Even today, as you enter the crypt under the church a strange atmospheric feeling surrounds you. There are strange goings on around here and several people have experienced the supernatural in this abnormal place.*

THE FACTS

Distance - 9 miles/14½ km
Time - 4 hours
Start - Hutton le hole grid ref. 704903
Maps - OS Landranger 94 or OS Outdoor Leisure 26
Terrain – Moorland paths, stony at times
Refreshments - Forge Tea Rooms at Hutton le Hole

The Route

S tart at the car park in Hutton le Hole and turn right up the hill away from the village. In a few yards at the right hand bend in the road follow the public footpath sign off to the left. Continue along this path climbing all the way bearing right until you meet a private road. Turn left onto the road which is a public footpath then in a quarter of a mile leave the road where it bears left and follow the public footpath sign straight ahead onto the moor. This track takes you over Hutton Ridge climbing high onto Spaunton Moor. At times the moor is used for Grouse shoots. Please do not attempt to walk this route if shooting is in progress. You will easily see the beaters sweeping their way over the moor making the low flying Red Grouse unsuspectingly fly towards the guns. Beware! Shotgun pellets can be bad for your health! In about a mile the track joins a wider track at a 'T' junction and a wooden marker post.

Go right here to follow the public footpath all the way over Loskey Ridge which ends at the road. Turn left and head along to Rosedale Bank Top. At the Bank Top there are the remains of the old kilns. Don't miss the fantastic view into Rosedale almost 1000ft beneath you. Apart from mining, Rosedale was also famous for glass making in the 16th century, a Priory which was demolished in 1535 and its connections with the Romans. After your history tour of the mining relics cross the road and head south east across the track to Ana Cross on the horizon. Turn right at the cross onto a narrow path heading in a southerly direction. Continue straight on until you meet a wider track which leads across Spaunton Moor and across Lastingham Ridge. Keep walking south and in a couple of miles leave the moor through a gate leading to Lastingham village. At the 'T' junction turn right towards Hutton le Hole.

Don't forget to visit the church and the old pub. Continue along the quiet road eventually turning right at the junction to cross over the bridge. Keep to the wide grass verge, perhaps cooling your tired feet in Loskey Beck along the way. In about a mile turn left through the trees on the footpath for a pleasant walk back to Hutton le Hole passing nearby to the Ryedale Folk Museum. At the village turn right, then right again to return to the car park.

Ana Cross

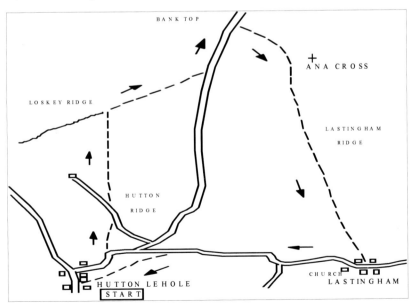

ALONG THE RIVER DOVE

*T**he** River Dove flows through Farndale taking its water from Westerdale, Baysdale and Farndale Moors. It is often known as the daffodil river because in the spring daffodils cover its banks in their thousands. The walk is only short and uses good paths from Low Mill to High Mill where refreshment is available at the 'Daffy Caffy' or the Feversham Arms at Church Houses. Before either returning along a quiet road of retracing your steps along the river bank.*

- - - o 0 o - - -

THE FACTS

Distance - 3½ miles/5 km
Time - 1½ hour
Start - Free small car park at Low Mill, grid ref. 673952
Maps - OS Landranger 94 or OS Outdoor Leisure 26
Terrain - Easy walking on good paths across fields
Refreshments - Daffy Caffy at High Mill, Feversham Arms a little further along at Church houses

- - - o 0 o - - -

The Route

You must make an early start on this walk as the small car park is soon full and there is nowhere else to leave your car. Leave the car park turning right then sharp right again through a small gate at the sign for High Mill. At the bottom of the paddock cross the river and pass through two small gates bearing left.

Follow the river keeping straight ahead at all times passing through several gates and fields following the waymarks until in a little over a mile pass through two large stone gate posts. Bear left now over the river past two more gate posts and you will see High Mill in front of you with the Daffy Caffy welcome sign on the gate. Pass through the mill buildings calling for refreshment if required.

Keep straight ahead along the drive if you wish to visit the Feversham Arms. Along the drive you will see a signpost directing you into a field. The signpost reads 'Public Path to Cow Bank'. Cross the field to a small gate opposite and over the footbridge. Bear right now following the sign for Cow Bank. It is quite a slog up the two fields to the road but the view is worth it from the top and there is a seat for a rest. Turn left at the road to return to Low Mill. If you would rather not walk on this quiet road please return along the river the way you came.

Farndale

The Feversham Arms

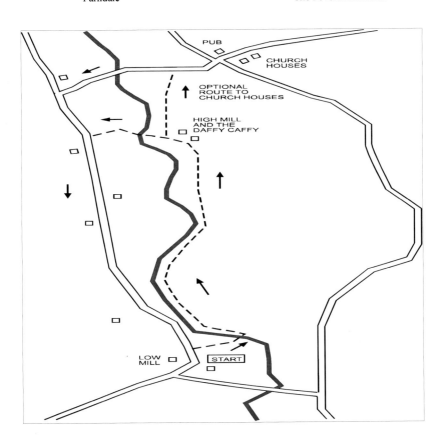

A WALK TO RUDLAND RIGG

*D*ividing the valleys of Bransdale and Farndale is the dominant ridge of Rudland Rigg. The high track over the top of the Rigg played its part in the industrial heritage of the area when ironstone mining was prominent. We reach the Rigg from Low Mill, a tiny community at the start of the daffodil valley of Farndale. This walk links the lush farmland of the sheltered valleys to the bleak nakedness of the Rigg with incredible scenery along the way.

Rudland Rigg was part of an ancient highway between Kirkbymoorside and Stokesley. Not only cattle drovers used the route but waggoners buying and selling farm produce to and from the markets were still using the road in the early 1900's. The road from the village of Fadmoor to Rudland Rigg was called Waingate which is Anglo Saxon for waggon road. The surface over the Rigg is a good example of a medieval road being in much the same condition now as it was a hundred years ago. Along the Rigg is to be found a huge stone, the 'Gammon Stone' which leans to one side. On that side is an inscription in Hebrew which means Hallelujah. The work is credited to the Reverend Strickland a local clergyman. The whole area around the Rigg was used for mining and half way along the Rigg is a crossing, Bloworth Crossing, where the mineral railway carried ore from the Rosedale and Farndale mines on its way to Teesside.

THE FACTS

Distance - 6½ miles/9 km
Time - 2½ hours
Start - Low Mill grid ref. 673952
Maps - OS Landranger 100 or OS Outdoor Leisure 26
Terrain - Rough moorland path
Parking - Small car park at Low Mill
Refreshment - Sandwiches & flask this time!

The Route

S tart from the small car park at Low Mill turning right onto the road and up the hill. In half a mile turn left along the road to Horn End signed as a bridleway to Rudland Rigg.

After the farm enter the field, take great care there might be the local Bull roaming with his concubines, and follow the path and waymarks which lead to a footbridge in about half a mile.

Cross the bridge and keep to the left following the line of the wall to a stile. Over the stile go diagonally uphill to the right following a worn track which soon bends sharp right and heads ever onwards and upwards through heather and bracken with confirmation waymarks along the way. When you reach a lonesome tree the path becomes undefined for a few yards. Keep right past the tree and you will soon pick up the path again heading uphill to the left. Climbing now past the shooting butts the path opens out to reach the wide track across Rudland Rigg. Turn right now then shortly turn right again at the sign prohibiting cars and motorcycles to leave the Rigg at this crossroad of tracks. Continue down off the moorland through the old mining area to the road at Monket House. Enjoy the fantastic view into Farndale as you descend. Turn right at the road then in a few yards go straight on at the junction following the sign for Low Mill back to the car park.

View From Rudland Rigg

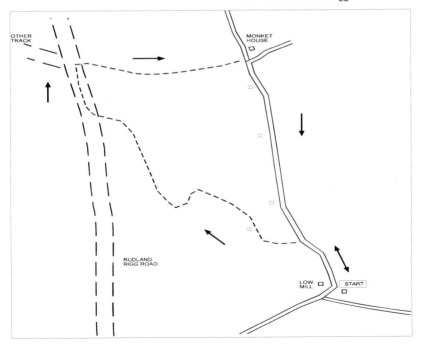

THE RIDGES & RIGGS AROUND FARNDALE

Starting from the Blakey junction of the old ironstone railway the walk follows the old track all the way to Bloworth crossing. The ironstone industry started in 1339 but it wasn't until 1861 that the railway was extended to Bloworth to carry ore to industrial Teesside. At Bloworth the railway track meets the route of a medieval road traversing the top of Rudland Rigg where we walk for the return leg. The walk circumnavigates Farndale, giving exhilarating views along this fascinating valley of the River Dove.

THE FACTS

Distance - 13.5 miles/21.7 km

Time - 6 hours

Start - start from the roadside car park area at Blakey Ridge near Hutton le Hole, grid ref. 684989

Maps - OS Landranger 94. OS Outdoor Leisure 26

Terrain - Flat grassy paths and undulating stony track. Very steep return route on quiet road

Refreshments - The Feversham Arms at Church Houses. The Lion Inn at Blakey

The Route

There is a parking area at the side of the road 6 miles (9.6km) north of Hutton le Hole on the Castleton road at the Farndale junction. Leave the car park, cross the road to the junction. Take this road towards Farndale then turn immediately right onto a wide track towards a gate welcoming walkers onto estate land. The wide track is clearly the path of the old ironstone railway which follows the contours along the side of Blakey Ridge and Farndale Moor. Evidence of mine workings are to be seen alongside the old railway and it was on these high moors that workers were trapped in a blizzard whilst building the line. They sheltered in huts which were completely covered by snow. As the track bends and turns the scenery changes and becomes wilder reaching a gate to a crossroad. The Ironstone Railway track heads straight on but it is here where you must turn left onto the medieval road across Rudland Rigg. Keep straight ahead across the Rigg on the wide, stony road. In a little over a mile on the top of a hill you will see a large sloping stone on your left. This is the Cammon Stone with a Hebrew inscription said to have been erected and carved by an eccentric clergyman. The view into Farndale was lost some time ago but is now replaced by the magnificent dale of Bransdale to the west. In about 1.5 miles another stone appears on the left, this time a guide stone with the inscription telling you that you are on the 'Kerby Rode'. In 0.5 miles from this stone at the bottom of the hill another track crosses your path with a vehicle restriction notice at the entrance. Leave the medieval road here to turn left along the track towards Farndale. Pass through the old mine workings and exit onto the road near Monket House turning right. In 100yds. Just past the house turn left at the road junction signed to Church Houses and Castleton. After crossing the bridge over the River Dove you soon arrive at Church Houses and the Feversham Arms for some refreshment. On leaving the village take the Castleton Road then bear left again signed to Castleton. It is a steep climb back to the main road at Blakey now but rewarding with fantastic views into Farndale. At the top of the hill cross the road to the car park.

Bransdale

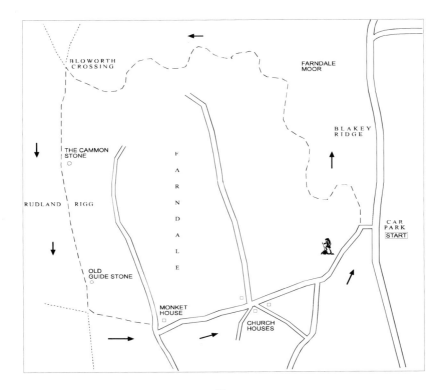

TRAILBLAZER BOOKS
CYCLING BOOKS
Mountain Biking around the Yorkshire Dales
Mountain Biking the Easy Way
Mountain Biking in North Yorkshire
Mountain Biking on the Yorkshire Wolds
Mountain Biking for Pleasure
Mountain Biking in the Lake District
Mountain Biking around Ryedale, Wydale & the North York Moors
Exploring Ryedale, Moor & Wold by Bicycle
Beadle's Bash – 100 mile challenge route for Mountain Bikers

WALKING BOOKS
Walking into History on the Dinosaur Coast
Walking around the Howardian Hills
Walking in Heartbeat Country
Walking in Captain Cook's Footsteps
Walking the Riggs & Ridges of the North York Moors
Short Walks around the Yorkshire Coast
Walking on the Yorkshire Coast
Walking to Abbeys, Castles & Churches
Walking around the North York Moors
Walking around Scarborough, Whitby & Filey
Walking to Crosses on the North York Moors
Walks from the Harbour
Walking in Dalby, the Great Yorkshire Forest
Ten Scenic Walks around Rosedale, Farndale & Hutton le Hole
Twelve Scenic Walks from the North Yorkshire Moors Railway
Twelve Scenic Walks around the Yorkshire Dales
Twelve Scenic Walks around Ryedale, Pickering & Helmsley

DOING IT YOURSELF SERIES
Make & Publish Your Own Books

THE EXPLORER SERIES
Exploring Ryedale, Moor & Wold by Bicycle

YORKSHIRE BOOKS
Curious Goings on in Yorkshire
The Crucial Guide to Crosses & Stones on the North York Moors

Visit Us Online at **www.trailblazerbooks.co.uk**